OUR NATIONAL PARKS

# Mount Rainier
# Mount McKinley
# Olympic

WITH

CRATER LAKE   LASSEN VOLCANIC   LAVA BEDS
CRATERS OF THE MOON   KATMAI

*by Frances Wood*

*Illustrated with photographs in color*

FOLLETT PUBLISHING COMPANY   CHICAGO

*Library of Congress Catalog Card Number: 64-15636*

123456789

*Union Pacific Railroad*

*Lofty, ice-clad Mount Rainier occupies
more than one-fourth of the park's 380 square
miles. This sweeping view of the ancient
volcano is from the Sunrise area.*

2

A tour of Mount Rainier, Mount McKinley, and
Olympic National Parks provides a memorable visit
to rugged mountain slopes, impressive glaciers, and
a rain forest. Unusual birds and animals inhabit
these natural wonders. Illustrated with beautiful
color photographs.

# Mount Rainier National Park

The Cascade Range is a rugged, highly scenic range of mountains running through Washington and Oregon into northern California.

Many of the snowcapped peaks in the range are ancient volcanoes. Three of these volcanic peaks—Mount Rainier, in central Washington; Crater Lake, in southern Oregon; and Lassen Peak, in northern California—are preserved in national parks.

Beautiful Mount Rainier is the highest of these peaks. It rises 14,410 feet into the sky, and was probably 2,000 feet higher before a series of small volcanic eruptions blew the top off ages ago.

*Bob and Ira Spring*

*Masses of wildflowers carpet the park's alpine meadows, over 5,000 feet up the mountains. The flowers are best in July and August.*

Even during the summer, Mount Rainier is nearly covered with snow and ice. This white mantle includes 26 glaciers that occupy about 40 square miles of mountainside. The Nisqually Glacier, on the south side of the mountain, and the Emmons, on the northeast side, are the best known and most easily reached of the 12 large glaciers. Paradise Glacier is the best known of the 14 small ones.

The glaciers, fed by the heavy annual snowfall and by avalanches of snow and ice, creep very slowly down the mountain; Nisqually, for example, travels about 200 feet a year. Glacial growth or shrinkage is controlled by climate. Several glaciers on Mount Rainier are now growing.

Pushing to the edge of the mountain snow, wildflowers in alpine meadows paint the landscape with vivid colors. These mountain "parks" lie above the forests, and their flowers sprout and bloom quickly in the brief growing season. Over 650 wildflower species have been counted in the park, many blooming in the lowlands from May to September.

SEWARD PENINSULA

Nome

Norton Sound

Yukon River

Fairbanks

MT. McKINLEY
+20320

Fort Yukon
8 mi. N of
Arctic Circle

ALASKA

BOUNDARY LINE USA CANADA

Mackenzie Bay

Mackenzie River

Canol

Dawson

YUKON
TERRITORY

DISTRICT OF
MACKENZIE

NUNIVAK
ISLAND

Kuskokwim
Bay

ALASKA
HIGHWAY

Anchorage

Seward

Cook Inlet

Gulf of Alaska

ALEXANDER ARCHIPELAGO

Haines Jct.

Whitehorse

Bering Sea

Bristol Bay

KODIAK
ISLAND

Haines

Juneau

BRITISH COLUMBIA

ALASKA PENINSULA

KATMAI
NATIONAL
MONUMENT

QUEEN
CHARLOTTE
ISLAND

Hecate Strait

Prince Rupert

ALEUTIAN
<ISLANDS

Queen
Charlotte
Sound

1

97

Pacific Ocean

VANCOUVER ISLAND

Strait of Georgia

Vancouver

Bellingham

97

Mount Rainier,
Mount McKinley,
and Olympic
National Parks

MT. OLYMPUS
+7954

Seattle

Olympia

MT. RAINIER
+14410

99

Portland

Columbia River

The dense evergreen forests in the lowlands are dominated by red cedar, western hemlock, and Douglas fir. Alpine firs, mountain hemlock, Alaska cedar, and white pine grow on the mountain slopes.

Nisqually, in the southwest corner, is one of the park's main entrances. The road from it leads to park headquarters and National Park Inn at Longmire, and to Paradise Valley, home of famous Paradise Inn. The valley is a center of park activity. Horseback trips go out from here, as do guided hikes on glacial ice hundreds of feet thick. One trip crosses Paradise Glacier to a dazzling ice cave.

*A girl rappels down an ice cliff on Mount Rainier's Winthrop Glacier.*

*Bob and Ira Spring*

7

*A chain of hikers in pants with rein-*
*forced plastic seats coasts down a gla-*
*cier slope. "Tin pants sliding" is a*
*popular sport at Paradise Valley.*

Leaving Paradise, the automobile road winds through scenic Stevens Canyon to Ohanapecosh, a park activity center. Then it turns north and joins the Mather Memorial Parkway, which enters the park at the northeast corner. A road branching off the parkway goes to the Sunrise area, where Sunrise Lodge serves meals but has no overnight facilities.

Visitor centers are at Sunrise, Longmire, and Ohanapecosh, and improved campgrounds are maintained at these three places and elsewhere in the park. Several primitive campgrounds are located on wilderness trails.

Mount Rainier's 300 miles of trails lead to many scenic spots near the activity centers, and wind through the park's great wilderness areas to glaciers, lakes, waterfalls, high peaks, and alpine meadows.

The 90-mile Wonderland Trail, for hikers and horseback riders, encircles the mountain. The complete trip takes hikers a week or more, and shelter cabins, spaced eight to twenty-one miles apart, are along the way. Shorter hikes can be made on the trail, since it occasionally intersects the road.

Wildlife is abundant in the park. Raccoons, Douglas squirrels, chipmunks, and marmots are common. Less numerous are coyotes, bobcats, cougars, and fox. Bears, elk, and black-tailed deer sometimes appear along the roads and trails, and mountain goats are often seen on high ridges and crags.

9

*Two of Mount Rainier's three rounded peaks can be seen in this panoramic view from the Stevens Canyon Road, southeast of the mountain.*

*Union Pacific Railroad*

*Wizard Island (above) is really a volcano within a volcano, for it is the top of a volcanic cone thrust up from the crater floor by dying Mount Mazama. The spiny-backed island of Phantom Ship (right) resembles an old-fashioned sailing ship.*

10

# Crater Lake National Park

An unbelievably blue lake in the crater of an ancient volcano is the outstanding feature of Oregon's Crater Lake National Park. The lake, nearly 2,000 feet deep, is the deepest in the United States and the second deepest in the Western Hemisphere. It is surrounded by 20 miles of brightly colored lava cliffs and peaks, which rise 500 to 2,000 feet above its surface.

The volcano, called Mount Mazama, once towered at a height of more than 12,000 feet. But, about 7,000 years ago, a mighty eruption caused the summit to collapse into a deep crater. Rain and melting snow gradually filled the crater with water and formed the lake, which has no inlet or outlet.

*Southern Pacific Railroad*

# Crater Lake National Park

**NORTH ENTRANCE**

Pumice Desert

209

TIMBER CRATER
+7403

RIM DRIVE

**CLEETWOOD COVE**

Boat Landing

THE WATCHMAN
+8025

Wizard Island

MT. SCOTT
+8926

Phantom Ship

Sinnott Memorial

Crater Lake Lodge

Rim Campground

Llaos Hallway

Park Headquarters

Lost Creek

62

**VEST ENTRANCE**

The Pinnacles

Annie Spring

Castle Crest Wildflower Garden

Mazama

UNION PEAK
+7698

Annie Falls

62

Panhandle

**SOUTH ENTRANCE**

The park, which covers 250 square miles, can be entered from the north, the west, and the south. All three roads go to the 35-mile Rim Drive, which completely encircles the crater and offers many fine views of the lake.

Short, easy trails go to the tops of some of the peaks. One popular trail leads to The Watchman, a peak on the west rim of the lake. The fire lookout tower atop The Watchman provides a splendid view of the lake as well as the surrounding area.

One of the most spectacular views is offered from the Sinnott Memorial Overlook building on the southwest rim of the lake. Here visitors look through mounted field glasses at points of interest and hear talks on the lake's origin by members of the Park Service. This building is part of the visitor center in Rim Village.

Launches circle the lake for close-up views of the remarkably clear water, the crater, Wizard Island, and Phantom Ship. Short boat trips land on Wizard Island, where a trail goes to the crater at the summit. All boat trips start from the landing at the foot of Cleetwood Trail, on the north shore.

13

*The Pinnacles, thin spires of pumice, rise out of 200-foot-deep Wheeler Creek Canyon, six miles southeast of Crater Lake.*

*A winter-white mantle encircles Crater Lake.*

Fishermen can rent rowboats and tackle at the landing and go after the lake's rainbow trout and landlocked sockeye salmon.

Crater Lake Lodge, cabins, and a campground are at Rim Village. Other campgrounds are on the south and west entrance roads and on the road to The Pinnacles.

Near park headquarters, three miles south of Rim Village, is the Castle Crest Wildflower Garden. Here flowers are identified by labels.

Wildflower meadows and evergreen forests color the park's once barren mountain slopes. Many animals find shelter here—bears, deer, red fox, beavers, coyotes, chipmunks, golden-mantled ground squirrels, marmots, and pikas, which look like tiny rabbits. Unusual birds in the park include the Clark's nutcracker, Steller's jay, peregrine falcon, bald eagle, and golden eagle.

*Bob and Ira Spring*

*The setting sun tints Lassen Peak rosy-pink in this view from Manzanita Lake. A healing forest is slowly covering the volcano's lower slopes.*

# Lassen Volcanic National Park

Many remarkable volcanic exhibits are preserved in Lassen Volcanic National Park, which lies at the south end of the Cascade Range in northern California.

Attesting to the violence of past volcanic activity in the area are the remnants of old craters, cinder cones, lava fields, weird lava formations, and volcanic "plugs"—masses of very stiff lava that were pushed up and hardened in place.

The park's outstanding feature is 10,457-foot Lassen Peak, a dormant volcano that last erupted during 1914-21.

A paved highway gives access to most of the volcanic phenomena in the western half of the park, and connects the park's southwest entrance with the Manzanita Lake entrance, in the northwest corner.

Near the southwest entrance, the highway passes the Sulphur Works, an area of hot springs and steam vents. Between Emerald and Helen lakes, a trail leaves the highway and goes slightly more than one mile to Bumpass Hell. This thermal basin, with its bubbling mud pots, mud volcanoes, steaming springs, and turquoise pools, resembles Yellowstone's Norris Basin, except that it lacks true geysers.

Another trail, a little north of Helen Lake, offers an easy two-and-one-half-mile climb to the summit of Lassen Peak.

*Subterranean heat bubbles to the earth's surface in boiling mud pots, mud volcanoes, and steaming hot springs at Bumpass Hell.*

*Plant life is reclaiming the Devastated Area, littered with lava and debris left after a volcanic eruption and a mudflow.*

After passing Summit and Hat lakes, the highway goes through the Devastated Area. This wasteland was stripped of all life in 1915, when hot lava melted the snow on the northeast slope of Lassen Peak and caused a great mudflow.

From here, the highway goes to Chaos Jumbles, two and one-half square miles of jumbled lava rocks, the result of violent avalanches down Chaos Crags.

Near the northwest entrance is beautiful Manzanita Lake, where there are cabins, a lodge, store, and visitor center, featuring dioramas of the area's volcanic origins. Campgrounds are located here and at several other points along the road.

The eastern half of the park is a vast wilderness area. Over 100 miles of trails lead through evergreen forests and mountain meadows to volcanic formations and lakes well stocked with fish. A few short, unimproved roads lead to campgrounds.

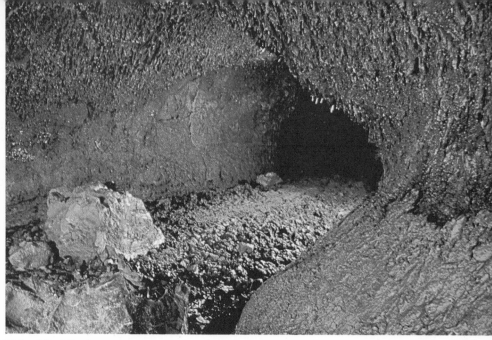

# Lava Beds National Monument

*Valentine Cave (above) and Catacombs Cave (below) are two of the many caves found in the 72 square miles of Lava Beds National Monument.*

The fantastic lava formations of Lava Beds National Monument tell an impressive story of ancient volcanic violence. This monument, in northern California near the Oregon border, is about midway between Crater Lake and Lassen Volcanic national parks.

18

Two types of volcanic eruption—explosive and fissure—occurred in the monument area.

The explosive eruptions hurled cinders, dust, and rock fragments into the air. These fell to earth, forming mounds, called cinder cones, around the vents through which they had been blasted. About 15 cinder cones are in the monument.

In the fissure eruptions, rivers of liquid lava flowed through fissures, or cracks, in the earth's surface. Often the surface lava in these rivers cooled quickly into a hard crust. Then the hot lava under the crust flowed away, leaving tubes and caves. Some of the tube roofs collapsed and left long, snakelike trenches. A few pieces of roof remained to form lava bridges.

In 1872-73, a small band of Modoc Indians, escaping from a reservation, took refuge in the winding trenches and caves. Fierce battles occurred, as the Indians resisted army forces for five months.

Visitors can explore this strange battleground, with its rock forts and cave hideaways, and can see the Indian paintings on some of the cave walls and bridges.

19

*These Indian petroglyphs, or rock carvings, are in a detached section of the monument, near Tule Lake.*

*A park ranger surveys Captain Jack's Stronghold, a lava-walled trench-fortress named after Captain Jack, leader of the Modoc Indians that fought United States soldiers from this maze of lava tubes and trenches.*

*Spatter cones, formed out of lumps of hardened lava, dot the barren, snow-covered landscape at Craters of the Moon National Monument.*

# Craters of the Moon National Monument

*Pahoehoe, or ropy lava, flowed peacefully over nearly half of the monument and hardened in rolling billows.*

Craters of the Moon National Monument is so named because its surface, covered with lava and pitted by shallow craters, somewhat resembles telescopic views of the surface of the moon.

The monument covers 83 square miles in southern Idaho, and contains one of the most varied displays of volcanic action. Lava is found in many forms—in cinder and spatter cones, flows, tubes, caves, bridges, lacy froth, and tree molds.

The lava in most of these formations erupted through the Great Rift, a series of fissures, or cracks, extending the length of the monument. Authorities believe these eruptions took place during the last million years, in three different periods of activity, and probably ended about 2,000 years ago.

20

*An aerial view of the monument's pitted surface.*

# Olympic National Park

Olympic National Park is one of the nation's big wilderness parks. It occupies nearly 1,400 square miles of the Olympic Peninsula, in northwest Washington, and contains the Olympic Mountains, highest in the Coast Range. Here are the mountain delights of glaciers, lakes, streams, waterfalls, and flowered meadows; here, too, are hot springs, ocean beaches, abundant wildlife, and unique and luxurious rain forests.

*National Park Concessions, Inc.*

*Lake Crescent Lodge overlooks lovely Lake Crescent, at the foot of Storm King Mountain. Cabins and campgrounds are also available.*

A jumbled mass of high ridges and peaks, the Olympics nearly fill the park and spill over its eastern edge. Mount Olympus, the loftiest peak, is 7,965 feet high; a number of other peaks are over 7,000 feet. Ridges climb to between 5,000 and 6,000 feet, and run in every direction. Between them lie low valleys, often less than 500 feet above sea level.

Excessive precipitation west of the mountains and on their western slopes brings about two results: glaciers in the mountains and lush rain forests in the valleys. Over 200 inches of precipitation—mostly snow—fall on the high country each year. Some of it accumulates from year to year, compresses into ice, and forms glaciers. Most of the 60 glaciers in the Olympic Mountains are small, but three on Mount Olympus are over two miles long.

A fine place to view the mountains is Hurricane Ridge, in the park's northeast corner. Reached by a paved road from Port Angeles, this area has trails through choice fields of wildflowers and to high overlooks. A day lodge with wide windows commands a sweeping view of the mountains.

A different world exists in the coniferous rain forests, in the low valleys to the west and south. Fed by an annual precipitation of 140 inches and more, trees grow to mammoth size; mosses, ferns, and wildflowers mat the forest floor and drape the trees; even the atmosphere seems to have a faint green tint.

23

*Flanked by snowcapped ridges and peaks, majestic Mount Olympus (center) looks like a fit "home for the gods." This view is from Hurricane Ridge.*

*Wash. St. Dept. of Commerce*

Sitka spruce, western hemlock, Douglas fir, and western red cedar are the coniferous trees of the rain forests; some of them grow 300 feet tall and eight feet thick, and are among the world's largest living trees. The best rain forests are in the Hoh, Queets, and Quinault valleys, all reached by good roads and penetrated by foot trails. A paved road goes 19 miles up the Hoh River and has a visitor center and radiating footpaths at its end.

More than 600 miles of trails reach all parts of the park. They range from short, self-guiding nature paths to long, strenuous mountain trails with overnight shelters.

24

*Visitors survey the Hoh Rain Forest. The sun, filtering through the treetops, fills the silent forest with a greenish-white light.*

In the park, 56 kinds of mammals have been counted. Deer, bear, and the famous Roosevelt elk are often seen, as are such small animals as raccoons, skunks, and, in the mountains, Olympic marmots.

A narrow strip of the Pacific Coast, 50 miles long, belongs to the park, although separated from it. Wild and unspoiled, this area offers fine beaches and interesting hiking along an often rocky coastline. Seabirds nest on offshore rocks and islands, and seals bask there.

U.S. Highway 101 encircles the park, and many branch roads enter the park from it; some are paved, some not. Campgrounds are along most of them.

U.S. 101 goes through Port Angeles; just out of town are park headquarters and a visitor center, the Olympic Pioneer Memorial Museum. The highway continues west along the south shore of beautiful Lake Crescent, where a visitor center, hotel, cabins, and other guest facilities are located. West of the lake, a 12-mile paved road goes to Sol Duc Springs, with a pool and cabins. Overnight facilities are also at Port Angeles and along U.S. 101.

25

*The famous Blue Glacier's blue-tinted ice extends down Mount Olympus for about two miles.*

*Wash. St. Dept. of Commerce*

*Densely forested ridges and snow-capped peaks form a dramatic background, as a deer grazes in a mountain meadow.*

*Bob and Ira Spring*

Bob and Ira Spring

*A cow moose drinks, as dawn tints mighty Mount McKinley.*

# Mount McKinley National Park

Mount McKinley National Park, in south-central Alaska, holds in its rectangle 120 miles of the Alaska Range, a mountain system that nearly fills Alaska's southeast quarter. Its heights are crowned by 20,320-foot Mount McKinley, highest mountain in North America.

North of the Alaska Range is a wide intermountain valley, and north of it are the low mountains of the Outside Range. The intermountain valley is crossed from north to south by river valleys, separated by ridges of 4,000 feet and higher.

The park road runs for 90 scenic miles through the intermountain valley, crossing river valleys and climbing over ridges.

Large glaciers lie on the south slope of the Alaska Range, where snowfall is heaviest. On the north slope are small valley glaciers and a few big ones fed by the highest mountains.

Much of the park is underlaid with permafrost, rock-hard frozen earth that never thaws. The summer sun thaws a few inches of topsoil, and plants grow in it; but their roots cannot penetrate the permafrost below.

Permafrost and bitter winters have resulted in treeless tundra throughout much of the intermountain valley and along the hillsides. The tundra is painted by thick mattings of moss and red and yellow lichens and, in summer, by wildflowers—forget-me-nots, lupines, wild peas, and others. At lower levels and on sun-warmed slopes, it supports hardy shrubs, among them dwarf birches and many kinds of willows.

*Wolfe Worldwide Films*

*A patch of scraggly spruce trees grows along the tundra edge.*

*Stewart's Photo Shop*

*The fox is one of the many animals in this vast wildlife refuge.*

*Wolfe Worldwide Films*

27  *Muldrow Glacier, on Mount McKinley's northern slope, is the largest glacier in the intermountain valley. It starts between the mountain's twin peaks and extends almost to the park road, a distance of about 35 miles.*

*Bob and Ira Spring*

Spruce forests grow in some of the larger river valleys and on sheltered slopes. Cottonwoods, willows, aspens, and white birches grow along the rivers, too.

Many of the park's animals can be seen from the road. White Dall sheep, smaller than the Rocky Mountain bighorns, winter in the Outside Range. In summer, they move swiftly across the intermountain valley to the Alaska Range.

28

*Wonder Lake, the park's only large lake, is a popular stopover for the wandering herds of caribou.*

Caribou feed in the intermountain valley and on the mountain slopes; their main food is the tundra's caribou lichen, plus grasses, herbaceous plants, and willows in summer. About the first of July, herds of several thousand caribou migrate through the park to their summer feeding grounds and tundra areas farther north and west.

The largest animal in the park is the Alaska moose. It may weigh nearly three-fourths of a ton, with antlers five or more feet across. Moose prefer the spruce forests but often feed on the tundra and in the tundra ponds.

The grizzly bear, the park's largest meat-eater, roams all areas but is most often on the tundra. The grizzly stalks mice, parka squirrels, marmots, and larger animals, but grasses, roots, and berries are its main diet.

Animals commonly seen from the road are the red fox, porcupine, marmot, beaver, and snowshoe rabbit; rarely seen are the coyote, timber wolf, wolverine, and lynx.

Ptarmigans, the little grouse of the north, are among the very few birds wintering in the park. In summer, however, many birds come and nest on the open tundra. Some of them come far across open water: the long-tailed jaeger from islands near Japan, the golden plover from Hawaii. Hundreds of species come from the Americas.

*Dall sheep can usually be seen in summer on the slopes near Igloo Creek, about 30 miles from park headquarters. The small goatlike horns of these sheep identify them as ewes.*

Denali Highway parallels the park's east border and enters near its northeast corner. Denali connects with the Richardson Highway, and thus with the Alaska Highway. The Alaska Railroad enters the park's southeast corner.

Near the northeast entrance are park headquarters and the McKinley Park Hotel. Here begins the park road, with its many fine views of tundra, mountains, and glaciers. Eielson Visitor Center, 66 miles from the hotel, is a splendid viewing place for Mount McKinley and Muldrow Glacier. Several campgrounds are along the road, which leaves the park near Wonder Lake and ends shortly beyond the park border.

# Katmai National Monument

Wildly beautiful Katmai National Monument, on the Alaska Peninsula, is a still-active volcanic region. In 1912, it was torn by one of the most violent volcanic explosions in history. Pumice, rock, and white-hot ash were thrown from the earth at Novarupta Volcano, covering the land for miles; ash was blown by winds to all parts of North America. Six miles away, Mount Katmai's peak collapsed and sank, forming a deep crater. Steam rose through thousands of cracks in the ash-filled valley below Novarupta, later named The Valley of Ten Thousand Smokes. Only a few "smokes" remain today.

*Bob and Ira Spring*

31

*Mount Katmai and the jade-green lake in its crater are preserved in our largest national monument. Covering over two and one-half million acres, it is larger than any national park.*

*Alaska brown bears, sometimes weighing 1,500 pounds, are the world's largest meat-eating land animals. These bears, fishing for salmon in an Alaskan river, are similar to those found in Katmai.*

Visitors can reach Katmai only by boat or plane and can view it from one of these or from jeep-bus. Katmai is a true wilderness, its spruce forests and grasslands largely unmarked by trails. Camping is permitted anywhere in the monument, and fishing is fine.

The area's most famous animal is the huge Alaska brown bear. Also here are moose, wolf, lynx, otter, lemming, and snowshoe rabbit.

Many birds summer in the monument. Water birds frequent the lakes and seacoast. Bald eagles build their nests on lofty pinnacles, and whistling swans nest in the rivers and swamps of this remote refuge.